10 9 8 7 6 5 4 3 2 1

Copyright© 2022. All rights reserved.

No part of this publication may be reproduced, distributed, or transmitted in any form or by any means, including photocopying, recording, or other electronic or mechanical methods, without the prior written permission of the publisher, except in the case of brief quotations embodied in critical reviews and certain other non-commercial uses permitted by copyright law.

Although every precaution has been taken to verify the accuracy of the information contained herein, the author(s) and publisher assume no responsibility for any errors or omissions. No liability is assumed for damages that may result from the use of the information contained within. Your legal remedy, if any, is limited to the amount paid for this book.

First published 2022 with a non-exclusive licence from the authors to CHEETAH® Purrrrrrr Publishing, an imprint of CHEETAH® Toys & More, LLC (CHEETAH®).

ISBN-13: 978-1-7328369-9-0
ISBN:10: 1-7328369-9-0

Permission requests should be submitted to the publisher in writing via email at **info@mycheetahinc.com** or **paulettetrowers@yahoo.com.**

CHEETAH Toys & More, LLC
207 Main Street, 4th Floor
Hartford, CT 06016
USA

Port Antonio P.O.
Portland
Jamaica
876-909-6311 (WHATSAPP)
www.mycheetahinc.com

Authors: Paulette Trowers, Kristina Jaz
Editors: Fiona Porter-Lawson, Patricia Bryan
Song writer: Iain Taylor
Cover design: CHEETAH®
Publisher: CHEETAH®

TABLE OF CONTENTS

Dear CHEETAH family: 5

Chapter 1: A world of water 8

1.1 All about water 11
    Water, water, everywhere! 11

1.2 The water cycle 22

1.3 The colour is clear 33
    Clear or blue? 33

1.4 Water sounds 39
    Wet and noisy! 39

1.5 Pouring water 47
    Tip me over and pour me out 47

1.6 Water in motion 53
    Moving, floating and sinking 53

1.7 A watery home 62
    Splishing and splashing! 62

Chapter 2: Useful water 75

2.1 Life with water 79
    Wonderful water! 79

2.2 Taste-tastic! 87
    Delicious drinks 87

2.3 Feel the heat 93
    Hot and cold 93

2.4 From dirty to clean 101
    Scrub-a-dub! 101

2.5 Water fun 111
    Make a splash! 111

RESOURCES 122

Sight words activities 123

Dear CHEETAH® family:

Welcome to the first volume of the CHEETAH book of water! It is time to explore and discover the joys of water.

This brilliant study book is packed full of facts, activities, songs, and games on exciting full colour pages. Through exploration and play, the pupil's development will be encouraged and nurtured as they achieve a huge range of learning outcomes on the topic of water.

Each chapter begins with an introductory image, which a parent or teacher can use to stimulate discussion with the pupil. This allows the adult to gauge the pupil's interest in and present understanding of a topic. What an ideal basis to support further learning!

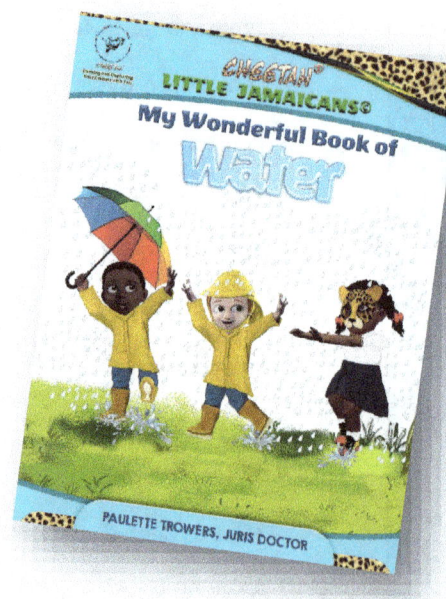

Key concepts are presented through engaging, illustrated text, followed by countless opportunities to apply new knowledge. Hands-on activities are outlined in detail, with cut-out pieces supplied. Adults can use these resources to create stimulating environments which motivate pupils to explore at their own pace.

Developmental goals central to the activities featured include motor coordination, understanding and appropriate use of language, respect for self and others, critical thinking, independent learning and coping skills.

This book also includes fun ways to reinforce sight words. At age five, children are expected to locate, say, and pronounce some sight words, so why not get a head start now? This book has songs throughout that introduce twenty of Dolch's words, included on his pre-primer list.

a	and	big	blue
come	find	go	in
is	it	little	look
play	red	see	the
to	we	yellow	you

Sight words

Did you know that some words in the English language occur much more frequently than others?

In the 1930s, Dr Edward William Dolch developed a list of the most frequently used words, which we still use today. These words make up over 50% of all written material! Memorising Dolch's list makes a big difference to the ease and fluency with which children learn to read. Being able to recognise instantly over 50% of the text they are reading allows children to focus on decoding unfamiliar words, without losing the meaning of the sentence. For this reason, Dolch's words are also known as **sight words**.

Look out for the magnifying glass (to spot the sight word moments), as you learn about water. At the back of this book, you will find flashcards of these words, along with some fun activities and games you can play with the pupil.

Ideas to extend learning also feature throughout the book—ideal for moments where the pupil is super excited by new discoveries!

Learning extension:
Head into the real world to look for these sources of water; you may find a tank and pipes near a building to show the pupil, or a river, the sea or a pond that you can go and visit. Stand in the rain! If the water is clean, encourage the child to feel it and get wet!

As you and the pupil read along together, the pupil will apply the CHEETAH® CAPE tool. Each section that contains this tool has a CAPE icon, like the one on this page.

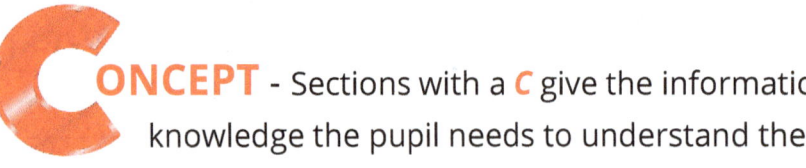

CONCEPT - Sections with a *C* give the information and knowledge the pupil needs to understand the chapter fully.

APPLICATION - Sections with an *A* ask the pupil to apply the information learned to solve a problem.

PRACTICE - Sections with a *P* allow the pupil to use the information and skills learned during fun activities that are guided by a parent or teacher.

EVALUATION - Sections with an *E* are a chance for the teacher and parent to communicate and keep track of the pupil's understanding of key concepts. This is also where the pupil will be given stickers to celebrate his or her learning!

Now it is time to enjoy a wonderful journey of discovery together!

Are you ready?

Chapter 1: A world of water

Words worth knowing

The list below contains the words from the curriculum that will be discussed within this chapter.

- bottom
- clean
- clear
- clouds
- dolphin
- drip
- dry
- empty
- fish
- float
- flow
- frog
- full
- jellyfish
- heavier
- lighter
- live

- pipe
- pond
- pool
- pour
- rain
- river
- sea
- shark
- shrimp
- sink
- sky
- tank
- top
- water
- wet
- whale

STOP Children will be using these words but should not be expected to spell or memorise them.

Let's talk!

What do you know about water?

How to support:
Look at the picture with the pupils and encourage them to tell you what they can see. Ask them to describe what is happening in different areas of the image. Scaffold with prompts such as, **'What is this? Why is this animal here? Where else is there lots of water?'**

Goal:
To have a better understanding of the pupils' existing knowledge about water. Use this knowledge to guide further learning and to complete the first column of the evaluation grid on the next page.

Evaluation grid

This evaluation grid is for teachers and parents. It will help you check the pupil's understanding of the concepts discussed throughout this chapter. Read each statement below and insert a check mark for concepts the pupil has already mastered before the chapter, and then after learning together.

The pupil understands...	Before this chapter	After this chapter
1. water can be found in many places (sea, river, pond, pool, tank, pipe)		
2. water falls from clouds as rain		
3. water has no colour; clean water is clear		
4. the colour blue is often used to represent water		
5. water makes things wet		
6. water makes many sounds, such as splashing, gushing, swishing, dashing, rumbling, roaring, dripping, gurgling, tapping and trickling		
7. we can pour water from one container to another		
8. we can estimate which container is heavier or lighter		
9. water can drip and flow		
10. water makes things move		
11. some things float on top of water while others sink to the bottom		
12. some animals (e.g. fish, crabs, frogs) and plants live in water.		

Look out for stars as you learn! These stars will show you which key concept is being taught.

1.1 All about water

In this section, the pupil will learn that:
- ✓ water can be found in many places (sea, river, pond, pool, tank, pipe)
- ✓ water falls from clouds as rain.

C Water, water, everywhere!

We live in a world full of water.

We can find lots of water in the sea.

Rivers are another place where we can find lots of water.

Have you ever visited a pond?

Ponds are full of water.

Look at this water flowing from a pipe.

Water can be found in tanks too.

Have you ever had a swim in a pool?

If you have, you were swimming in water.

Water also falls as rain from clouds in the sky.

Water is all around us!

A Where is the water?

Look at the place where you can find water and tick the word box to match.

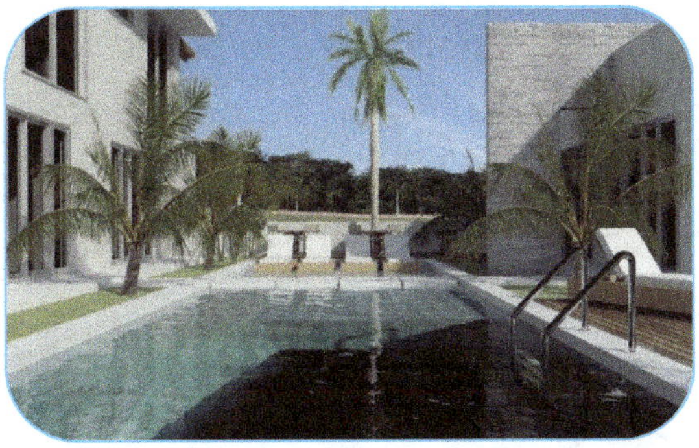

- [ ] sea
- [ ] pool
- [ ] river

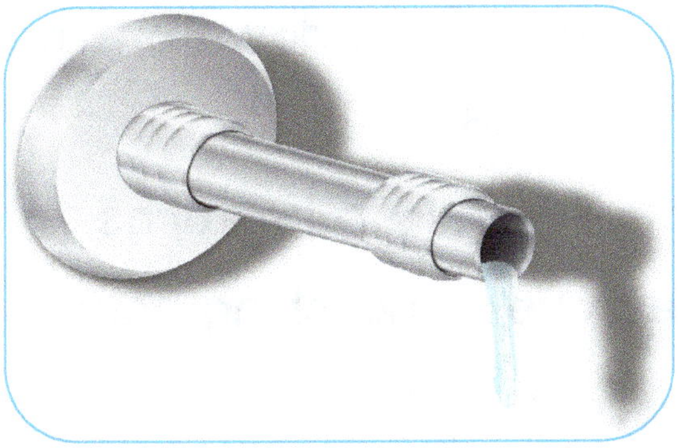

- [ ] tank
- [ ] rain
- [ ] pipe

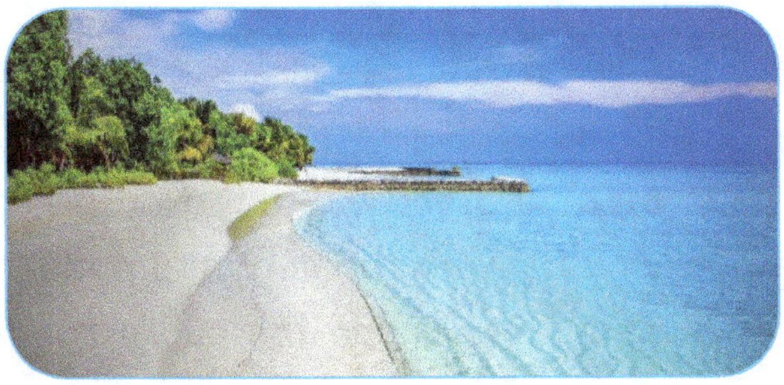

- [ ] pond
- [ ] sea
- [ ] tank

CHEETAH™ Toys & More, LLC Copyright 2022

 **Let me do it!**

Watery pairs

What you will need:
- child-friendly scissors
- watery pairs game cards (next page)
- the *and* sight word flashcard
- 2 players

How to support:
As you help the pupils cut out the cards, discuss: 'Where is the water in this picture?' This is a memory game, so be sure to encourage the pupils to remember where the pictures are, even if they don't win the pair. Ask, 'What did you turn over?' Encourage use of the word *and* in the pupils' responses, by laying out the first picture, the *and* flashcard and the second picture e.g. 'sea and river.'

1. Help the pupils cut out the cards.
2. Picture side down, the pupils should mix the cards.
3. Next, have the pupils lay the cards face down on the table or floor, with the pictures hidden.
4. With another player, each pupil should take turns to turn two cards over. If they are a matching pair, they take them away.
5. Whoever has the most pairs at the end of the game wins!

Learning extension:
Head into the real world to look for sources of water; you may find a tank and pipes near a building to show the pupils or a river, the sea or a pond that you can go and visit. If the water is clean, encourage the pupils to feel it and get wet. Stand in the rain.

Watery pairs game cards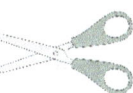

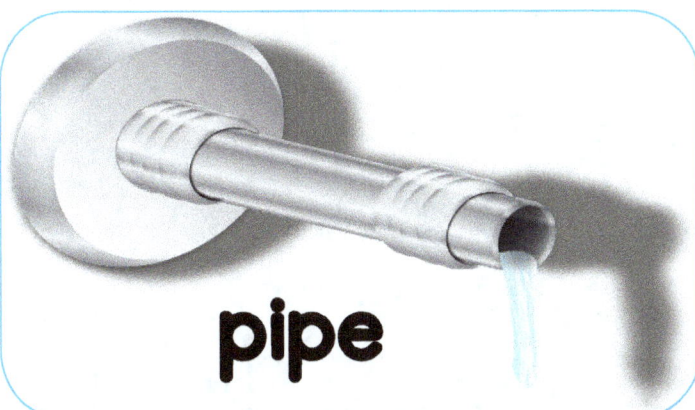 

This page has been left blank so you can cut out the picture cards. Remove the page first to make cutting out easier.

Watery pairs game cards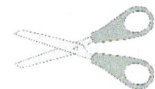

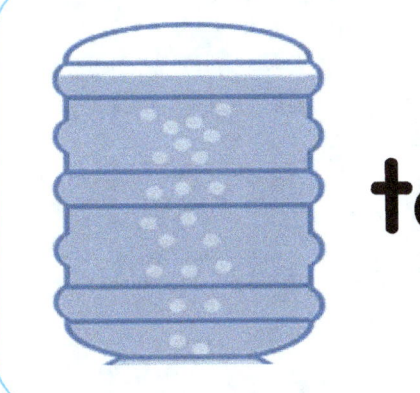 tank

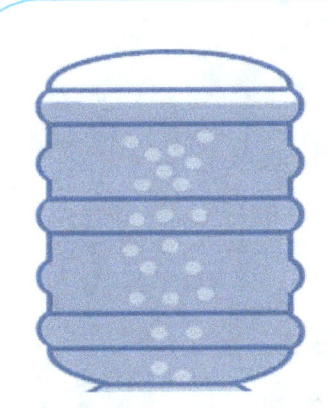 tank

 pond

 pond

 rain

 rain

This page has been left blank so you can cut out the picture cards. Remove the page first to make cutting out easier.

Water everywhere: How am I doing?

Date: _____

Dear Parent:

_____ does/does not fully understand that water can be found in many places (sea, river, pond, pool, tank, pipe) and falls from clouds as rain. Please review at home. Let us continue to work together.

Signed: _____

Date: _____

Dear Teacher:

Thank you. We have reviewed the concepts. My child had a chance to teach me.

Signed: _____

Sticker for mom and/or dad goes here!

Amazing!

_____
(write name here)

understands that water can be found in many places (sea, river, pond, pool, tank, pipe) and falls from clouds as rain.

Sticker for pupil goes here!

This page has been left blank so you can cut out the previous page.

1.2 The water cycle

In this section, the pupil will learn that:
- ✓ rain gives us water
- ✓ rain comes from the clouds in the sky.

C Water from where?

Water is all around us, but where does it come from?

Water comes from the sky as rain!

The water cycle describes how water goes from the sea, rivers and lakes to the air and back to the ground as rain.

Let us find out more!

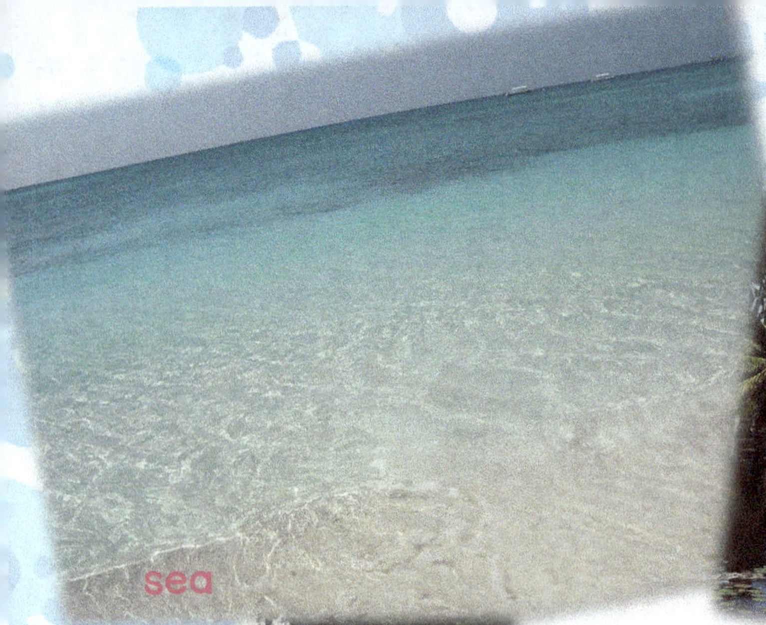

sea

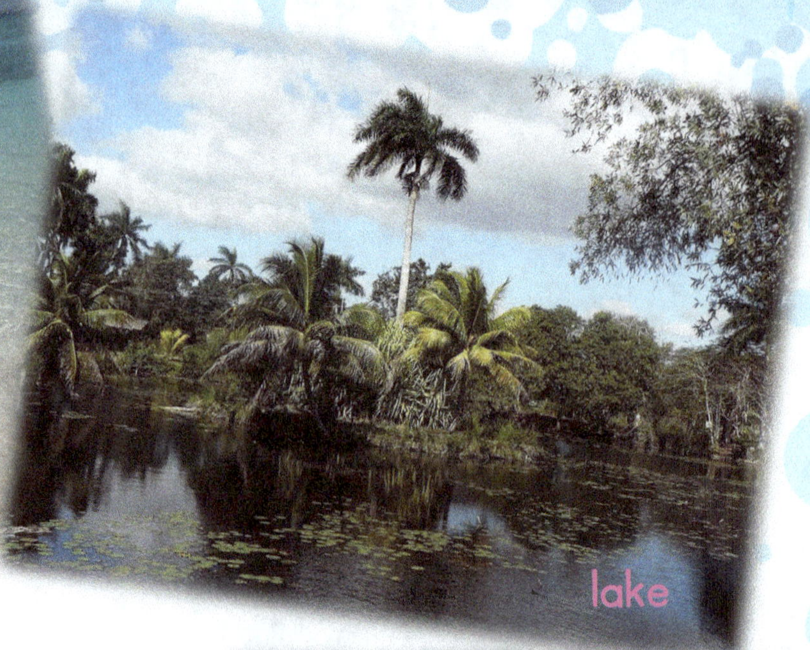

lake

river

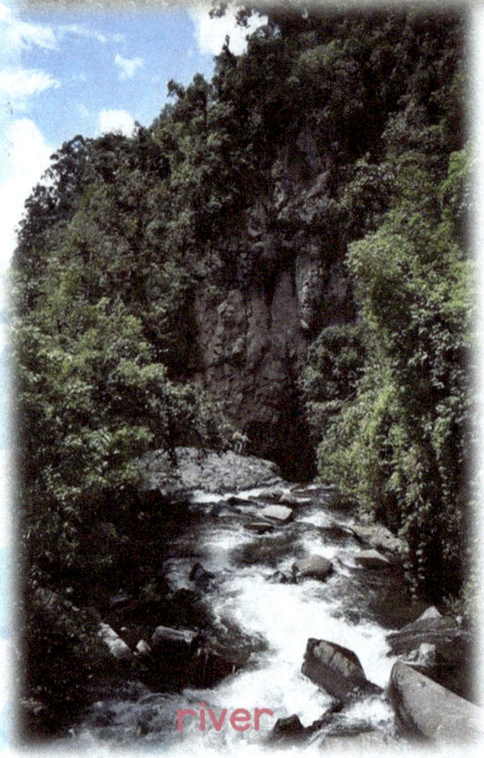

Water is in the sea, rivers, lakes, puddles and even in us!

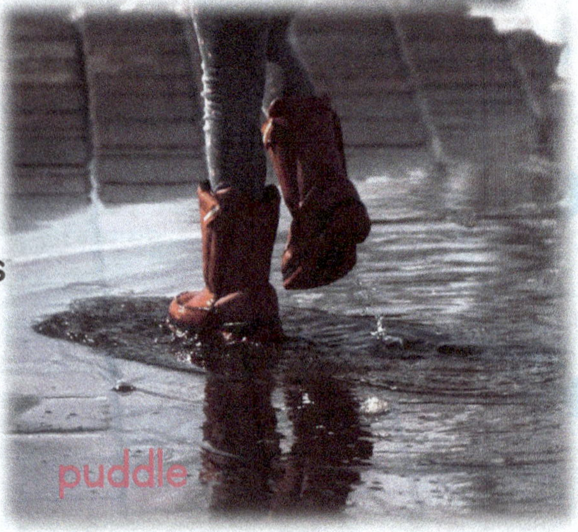

puddle

When the sun warms water, the water turns into water vapour.

You cannot see water vapour, but it is a gas that is all around us!

the sun warming the water

CHEETAH™ Toys & More, LLC Copyright 2022

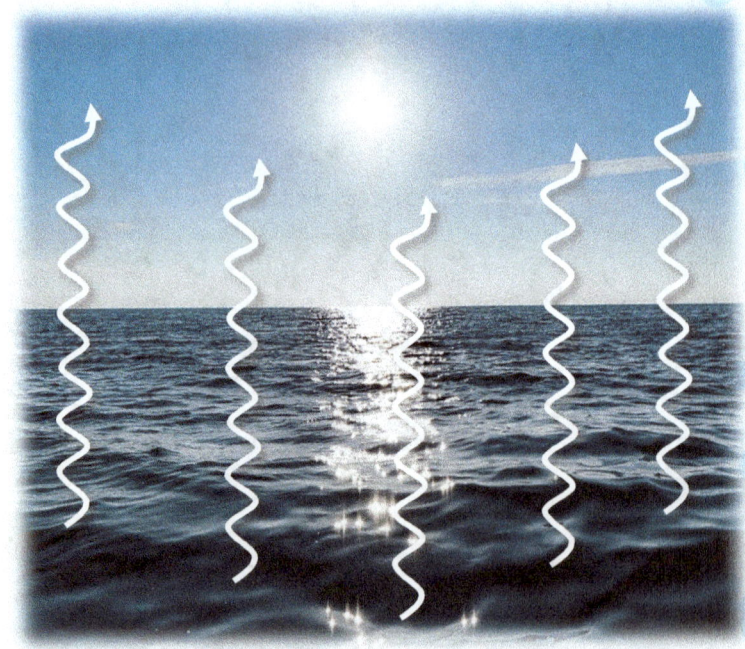

The warm sun makes the water vapour travel high into the sky.

clouds

It is colder all the way up there, so the water vapour cools down. As the water vapour cools, it forms clouds.

When enough water vapour has cooled, water droplets form.

water droplets

rain

The water droplets get so heavy, they fall as rain.

snow

If it is very cold, the water droplets fall as snow.

The rain or snow lands in the sea, in rivers and on the ground. Water on the ground makes puddles.

What do you think happens when the sun heats the water droplets that have fallen?

Let's see if you got the answer: the water cycle happens all over again!

A Where in the water cycle?

Cut out the images on the next page, then glue them onto the correct part of the water cycle.

Where in the water cycle? Cut out pieces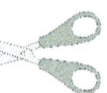

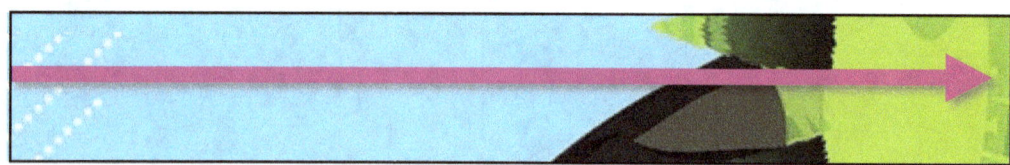

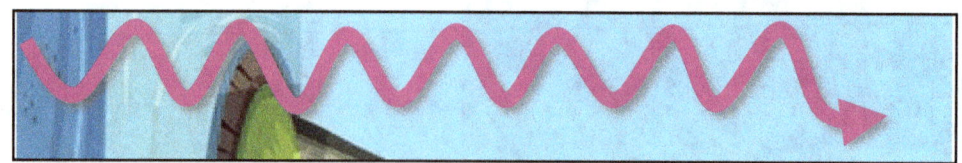

This page has been left blank so you can cut out the pictures. Remove the page first to make cutting out easier.

Let me do it!

Cycle in a bottle

What you will need:
- an empty, transparent water bottle (with a lid and the label removed)
- a marker
- water
- ice cubes

How to support:
Add colour to the water if you can. Talk to the pupils about the experiment as you are setting it up together, asking questions, such as, 'Where is the sea?' 'What do you think will happen to the water when we put the bottle in the sun?' or 'Why are the ice cubes there?'

1. Turn the water bottle upside down.
2. Use a marker to draw a wavy line for the sea. Draw the clouds in the sky, then draw the sun high above them.
3. Pour water into the bottle. Put the lid on top and turn it upside down again. Place ice cubes on top.
4. Put the bottle in a sunny place and watch what happens. Do you see a cloud form?

Learning extension:
Act out the journey of a raindrop, using instruments to accompany what is happening. Make a puddle outside and draw around it with chalk; return after ten-minute intervals to draw the new outline until the whole thing evaporates. Make a water cycle collage on a paper plate or circular piece of thick cardboard.

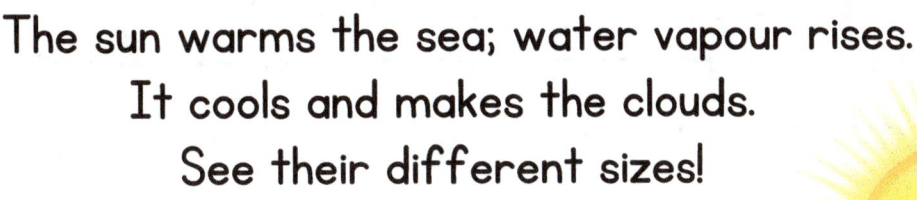

Let's rap: The water cycle song

The sun warms the sea; water vapour rises.
It cools and makes the clouds.
See their different sizes!

Raindrops form, just like that!
See the water falling back.
Pitter patter, look at how it flows.
Back into the sea it goes.

The sun warms the sea; water vapour rises.
It cools and makes the clouds.
See their different sizes!

Raindrops form, just like that!
See the water falling back.
Pitter patter, look at how it flows.
Back into the sea it goes.

You will need:
- the set of sight words flashcards
- paper or card and coloured pens

How to support:
Look at the flashcards together and support the pupils by reading them. Look at the page together – what clues do the pictures give us about the rap? Tell the pupils that reading the rap will give us more clues and read the words together. Do the pupils know what the rap is about? Have them sort the sight words cards into those found in the rap and those not found in the rap.

Learning extension:
Choose nouns from the rap to make extra flashcards. Draw a picture of each noun on the back of its card. Practise reading the new words, flipping the card over to see if the pupils are correct.

 The water cycle: How am I doing?

Date: _____

Dear Parent:

_____ does/does not fully understand that rain gives us water and comes from the clouds in the sky. Please review at home. Let us continue to work together.

Signed: _____

Date: _____

Dear Teacher:

Thank you. We have reviewed the concepts. My child had a chance to teach me.

Signed: _____

Sticker for mom and/or dad goes here!

Fantastic!

_____
(write name here)

understands that rain gives us water and comes from the clouds in the sky.

Sticker for pupil goes here!

This page has been left blank so you can cut out the previous page.

1.3 The colour is clear

In this section, the pupils will learn that:
- ✓ water has no colour; clean water is clear
- ✓ the colour blue is often used to represent water.

C Clear or blue?

What colour is clean water?

Is it orange, like orange juice?

Or white, like milk?

Turn a tap on and look!

What colour is the water?

Clean water does not have colour!

Clean water is clear.

Clean water is hard to draw, because it is clear.

This is why you will often see blue used to show water.

In this drawing of a duck in a muddy puddle, the rain and the puddle both show water as blue.

This drawing uses blue to show water in a glass.

The next time you read a book, look for blue water in the pictures.

A Colour me blue

Colour the water in the pictures blue.

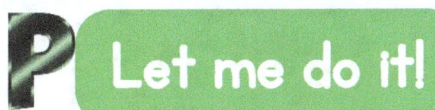

Let me do it!
Colour play!

What you will need:
- clear containers, with and without lids (e.g. empty squeeze bottles, drink bottles, bowls, beakers, etc.)
- access to clean water
- food colouring, or natural substances that will dye water (e.g. paprika, coffee, fruit/veg)

How to support:
This activity is best carried out outside. A hose can also make life easier when filling the containers. When the containers are first filled, ask the pupils, 'What colour is the water?' (clear). Ask again after the dye is added. Allow the pupils to experiment and get wet!

1. Have the pupils line up the containers and fill them to the top with clean water.
2. The pupils should add different food colouring (or natural dye) to each container. Ask them to observe what happens to the water.
3. For the containers that have lids, help the pupils to put them on and to shake each container. Ask the pupils to describe what happens.
4. Next, have pupils mix the water from one container with the water from a different container. Again, have the pupils observe what happens.
5. Give them time to try squeezing water, pouring water, dribbling water and splashing water!

Learning extension:
Before you begin the activity, show pupils the flashcards with the words *blue*, *red* and *yellow*. Stick them up nearby and, as you discover these colours together, draw the pupils' attention to the words.

The colour of water: How am I doing?

Date: _____

Dear Parent:

_____ does/does not fully understand that water has no colour; clean water is clear, and the colour blue is often used to represent water. Please review at home. Let us continue to work together.

Signed: _____

Date: _____

Dear Teacher:

Thank you. We have reviewed the concepts. My child had a chance to teach me.

Signed: _____

Sticker for mom and/or dad goes here!

Fantastic!

_____
(write name here)

understands that water has no colour; clean water is clear, and the colour blue is often used to represent water

Sticker for child goes here!

This page has been left blank so you can cut out the previous page.

1.4 Water sounds

In this section, the pupils will learn that:
- ✓ water makes things wet
- ✓ water makes many sounds, such as splashing, gushing, swishing, dashing, rumbling, roaring, dripping, gurgling, tapping and trickling.

C Wet and noisy!

Have you noticed that water makes things wet?

This dog is wet because it is splashing in the sea.

This wheel is wet because someone is washing it with water and soap.

Standing in the rain is making this boy wet.

Water makes things wet!

Did you know that water also makes different sounds?

Listen to them all!

trickling

gurgling

tapping

dripping

swishing

rumbling

Water makes loud sounds too!

splashing
dashing
gushing
roaring

A Sounds wet!

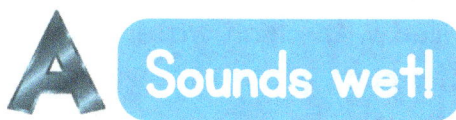

Trace the lines to match the water to the sound it is making.

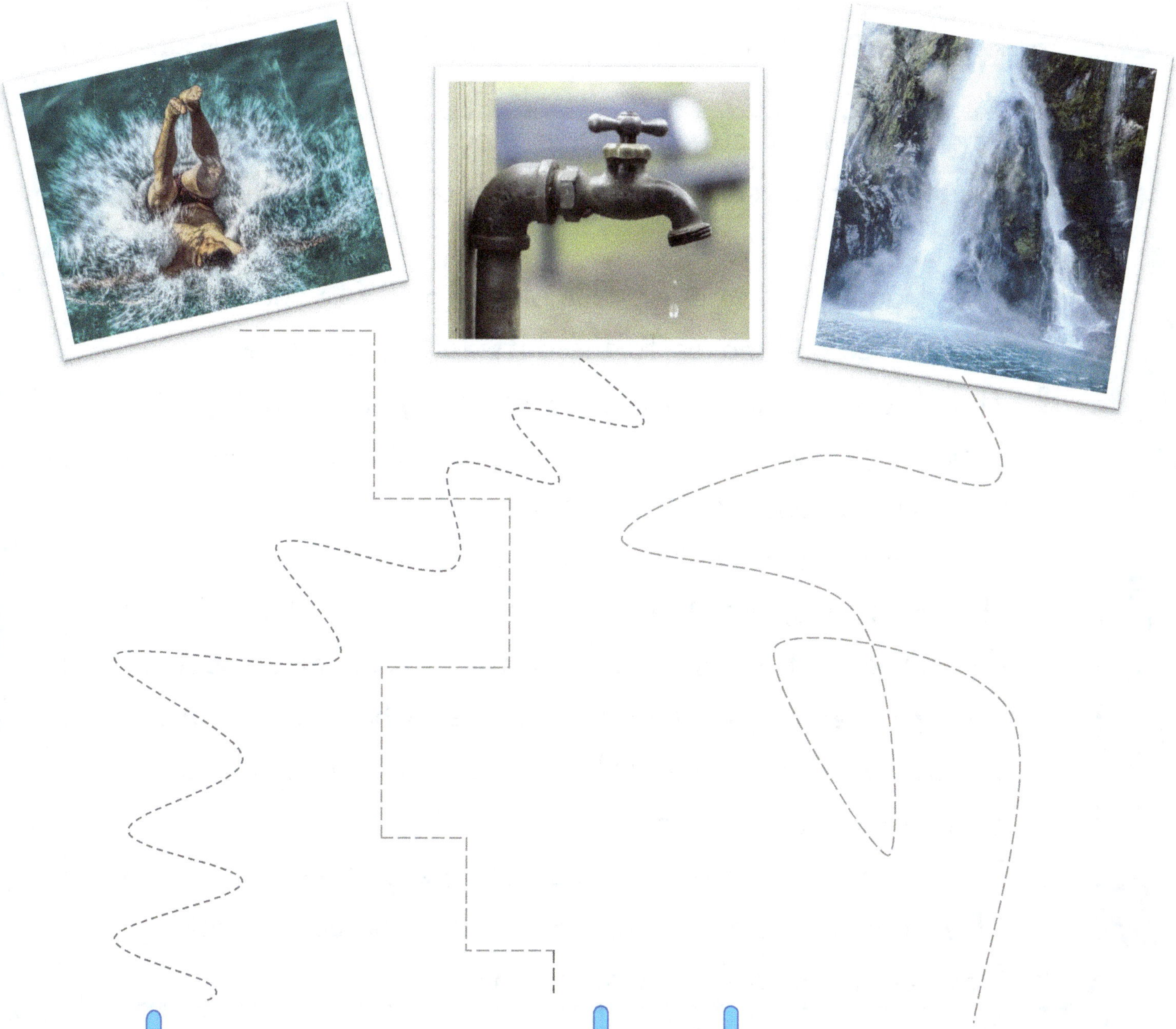

drip splash roar

CHEETAH™ Toys & More, LLC Copyright 2022

Let me do it!

Drip, drip, splash!

What you will need:
- a bucket (or other large container) half filled with clean water
- a plastic cup
- some towels
- P.E. or water play clothes

How to support:
Have a half-time break for the pupil to dry off, and play again using the words "trickle, trickle, DASH!" Be sure to talk about how the water is making everyone wet!

Have the pupils head outside. Divide them into small groups, then let each group sit on the ground in a circle around each bucket.

1. Select a player to be 'it'. This player half fills the cup with water and moves to the outside of the circle.
2. The player who is 'it' starts where they were sitting, dips their fingers in the cup of water, sprinkles a little on the next pupil's hands and says 'drip'!
3. Play continues around the circle, dripping water on each player's hands, until the player who is 'it' says 'splash' and drops the rest of the cup of water on someone's hands.
4. The splashed player chases the player who is 'it' around the circle, trying to beat them to sit back down in the splashed player's space.
5. The player who loses the chase scoops another half a cup of water and continues to play around the circle again.
6. Play continues until the water runs out!

Learning extension:
Set up containers for water play and support the pupils in using the water to make the sounds discussed in the chapter. Look for sounds made by water in the real world, around the home and by visiting a waterfall, a river or the sea.

Let's rap: What is it?

You'll find me in the sea,
in lakes and rivers and cups of tea.
I drip and drop and flow.
Without me, how would cruise ships go?

You'll find me in a pool,
and in the pipes at home and school.
I make our bodies wet,
and form the tasty drinks we get.

You will need:
- the *it* and *in* sight words flashcards
- two different coloured pencils

How to support:
Look at the *it* and *in* flashcards together. Ask, 'What is the same/different about these two words?' Look at the page together – what clues do the pictures give us about the rap? Tell the pupils that reading the rap will give more clues and read the words together. Do the pupils know what the rap is about? Have them circle all instances of *it* with one colour and *in* with another colour.

Learning extension:
What happens when other letters/sounds are added in front of the words *it* and *in*? Go through the alphabet with the pupils and see what other words they can make in this way!

Wet sounds: How am I doing?

Date: _____

Dear Parent:

_____ does/does not fully understand that water makes things wet and water makes many sounds, such as splashing, gushing, swishing, dashing, rumbling, roaring, dripping, gurgling, tapping and trickling. Please review at home. Let us continue to work together.

Signed: _____

Date: _____

Dear Teacher:

Thank you. We have reviewed the concepts. My child had a chance to teach me.

Signed: _____

Sticker for mom and/or dad goes here!

Great job!

_____
(write name here)

understands that water makes things wet and water makes many sounds, such as splashing, gushing, swishing, dashing, rumbling, roaring, dripping, gurgling, tapping and trickling.

Sticker for child goes here!

This page has been left blank so you can cut out the previous page.

1.5 Pouring water

In this section, the pupils will learn that:
- ✓ we can pour water from one container to another
- ✓ we can estimate which container is heavier or lighter.

C Tip me over and pour me out

Have you ever poured water?

We can pour water from a teapot into a cup,

from a jug into a glass,

or from one bucket into another bucket.

When water is poured into a container, the container gets heavier.

Look at this big watering can. When water is poured into it, it will become heavier.

This watering can is little. When water is poured into it, it will become heavier.

The little watering can will be lighter than the big watering can.

Do you know why?

lighter

heavier

Because we can pour more water into the big watering can!

A Heavier or lighter?

Circle the container that you think is **heavier**.

Let me do it!

Pour some more!

What you will need:
- a bucket (or other large container) half filled with clean water
- different sized/shaped containers
- a jug
- access to a tap
- towels
- the *big* and *little* flashcards

How to support:
Ensure that the containers you provide in the water-pouring station are made of non-breakable materials (i.e. plastic, paper, etc.) Keep refilling the bucket as necessary during the activity. Begin by modelling how to pour, then allow the pupils the freedom to explore pouring independently.

1. Set up a water-pouring station outside. It should have containers of different shapes and sizes, and at least one jug.
2. Discuss the range of containers on offer, with the pupils using the *big* and *little* flash cards to sort some containers according to size.
3. Show the pupils how to use the jug to scoop some water from the bucket and pour it into a container. Encourage the pupils to use both hands and take their time.
4. Allow the pupils to experiment with pouring water between different containers.
   - Can they pour using one hand then the other hand?
   - Can they pour into a little container?
   - Can they fill a container all the way to the top?
   - Can they pour without spilling a drop?

Learning extension:
During the activity, ask the pupils questions relating to estimating heavier/lighter. Add a floating object to the water in a container so they can watch it rise with the water level. Introduce the word *floating*. Develop fine motor skills by encouraging pouring into smaller containers.

Pouring water: How am I doing?

Date: _____

Dear Parent:

_____ does/does not fully understand that we can pour water from one container to another and estimate which container is heavier or lighter. Please review at home. Let us continue to work together.

Signed: _____

Date: _____

Dear Teacher:

Thank you. We have reviewed the concepts. My child had a chance to teach me.

Signed: _____

Sticker for mom and/or dad goes here!

Well done!

(write name here)

understands that we can pour water from one container to another and estimate which container is heavier or lighter.

Sticker for child goes here!

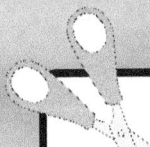
This page has been left blank so you can cut out the previous page.

1.6 Water in motion

In this section, the pupils will learn that:
- ✓ water can drip and flow
- ✓ water makes things move
- ✓ some things float on top of water while others sink to the bottom.

C Moving, floating and sinking

Have you ever watched water move?

Have you seen water flow in a river?

Have you ever seen water drip from a tap?

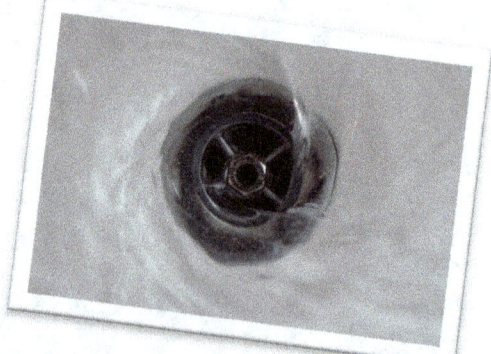

If you turn on the tap, you can watch water flowing down the sink.

When water moves, it can make other things move too.

Water is moving this man on a surfboard.

Water is moving this leaf.

Can you see how the leaf is sitting on top of the water?

Things that sit on top of water float.

Can you think of anything else that floats?

Boats, pool inflatables and water lilies all float on water!

Not all things float.

Some things sink to the bottom when they are in water.

Rocks and coins sink to the bottom when they are in water.

Some things float, and other things sink.

A Float my boat!

Cut out the boat and the rocks. Glue the boat **floating on top of the water,** and the rocks **sunk at the bottom of the water.**

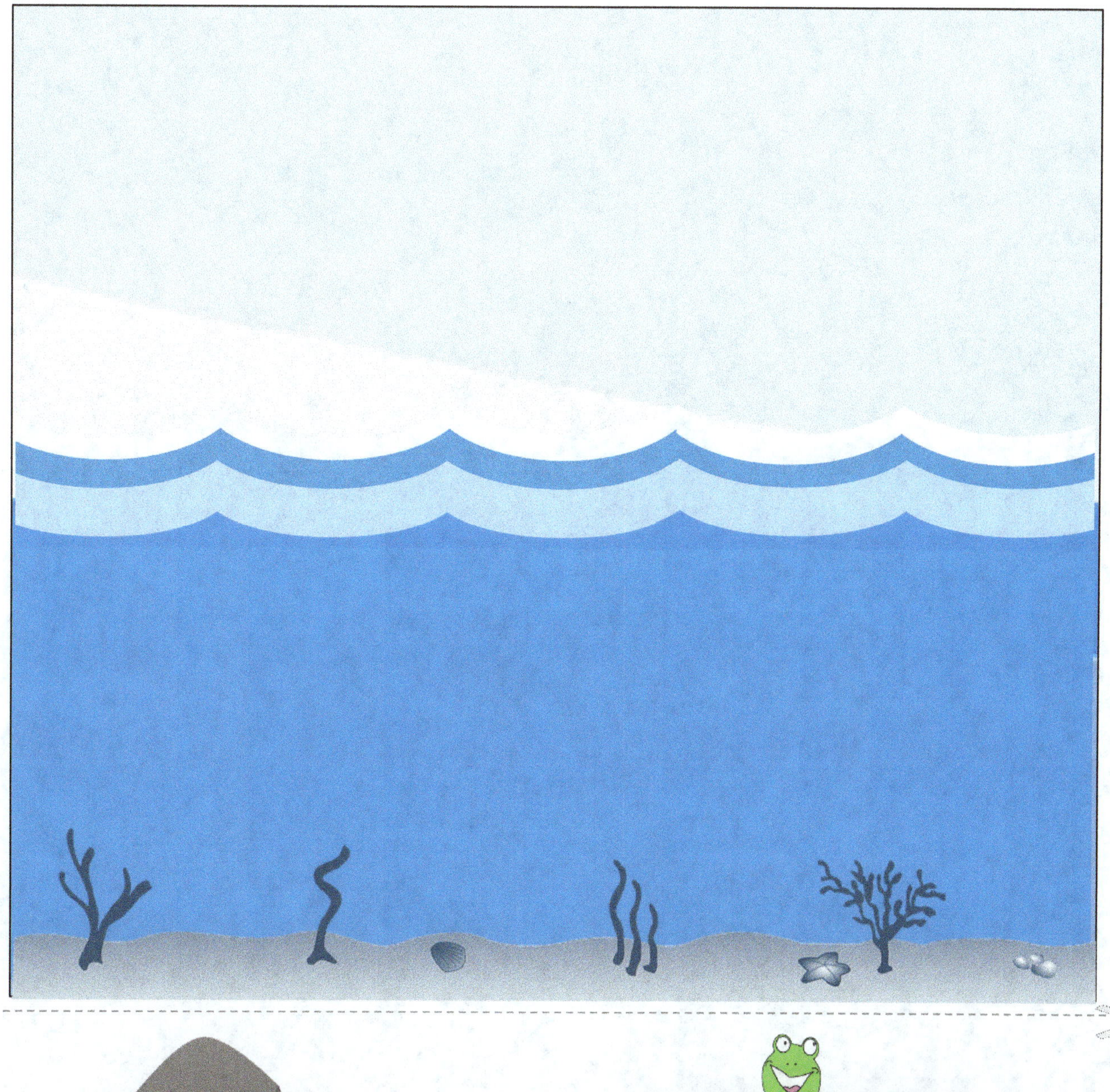

This page has been left blank so you can cut out the picture section. The rest of the page can stay in the book!

Let me do it!

Float or sink experiment

What you will need:
- a large, transparent container, half filled with water
- a variety of small items – some that float, and some that sink
- some towels

How to support:
Possible items that will float include sticks, corks, leaves, bathtub toys, sponges, crayons, drinking straws. Possible items that will sink include metal utensils, stones, coins, keys. Ask the pupils why they think certain objects will float/sink as they experiment. Celebrate correct predictions together and join the surprise when the pupils make new discoveries.

1. Help pupils to sort the items into two piles: one of items they think will float and the other of items that they think will sink.
2. Let them choose an item and drop it into the tub of water. Did it float or sink? Was their prediction correct?
3. Repeat step two with a new item.
4. Have pupils count how many of the items floated/sank when placed in water.
5. Can they find other items that will float/sink?

Learning extension:
Find a suitable video on the internet with a boat lowering its anchor. Watch it with the pupils. Place a toy boat (or other floating container) in water and ask the pupils how to make it sink. After the discussion, allow the pupils to test out their ideas to see which were effective.

P Let me do it!

A brilliant boat

What you will need:
- household rubbish e.g. plastic food tubs, cardboard boxes etc.
- glue/sticky tape
- child-friendly scissors
- craft materials e.g. paint, paper

How to support:
Encourage the pupils to use their existing knowledge to predict which materials would be best for making a boat. Help the pupils to make their boats when necessary, reminding them that any holes will let water inside – what would happen to the boat then? It is fun to take the boats to a stream/river to watch them moved by water, but if necessary, a hose on the ground, angled downhill to make a stream, can work just as well.

1. Explain to the pupils they will make a boat that water can move and discuss their ideas.
2. Let the pupils choose the materials they will use to build their boat. Encourage them to test what happens to the material when they put it in water – will this material be suitable?
3. Support the pupils in building and decorating the boat.
4. Have the pupils test their boat! Did the water make the boat move? Why/why not?

Learning extension:
Give pupils the opportunity to refine their boat based on how well the water moved it. How could they improve it? Have pupils design and build a boat for a grand boat race! Place a hose on the ground, angling it downhill to make a stream, and have the pupils observe small, light objects (such as leaves or flowers) move/float downhill with the flow of the water.

 **Water in motion: How am I doing?**

Date: _____

Dear Parent:

_____ does/does not fully understand that water can drip and flow; water makes things move; and some things float in water on top of water while others sink to the bottom. Please review at home. Let us continue to work together.

Signed: _____

Date: _____

Dear Teacher:

Thank you. We have reviewed the concepts. My child had a chance to teach me.

Signed: _____

Sticker for mom and/or dad goes here!

Excellent!

_____
(write name here)

understands that water can drip and flow; water makes things move; and some things float in water on top of water while others sink to the bottom.

Sticker for child goes here!

This page has been left blank so you can cut out the previous page.

1.7 A watery home

In this section, the pupils will learn that some animals (eg. fish, crabs, frogs) and plants live in water.

C Splishing and splashing!

Did you know some animals **live** in **water**?

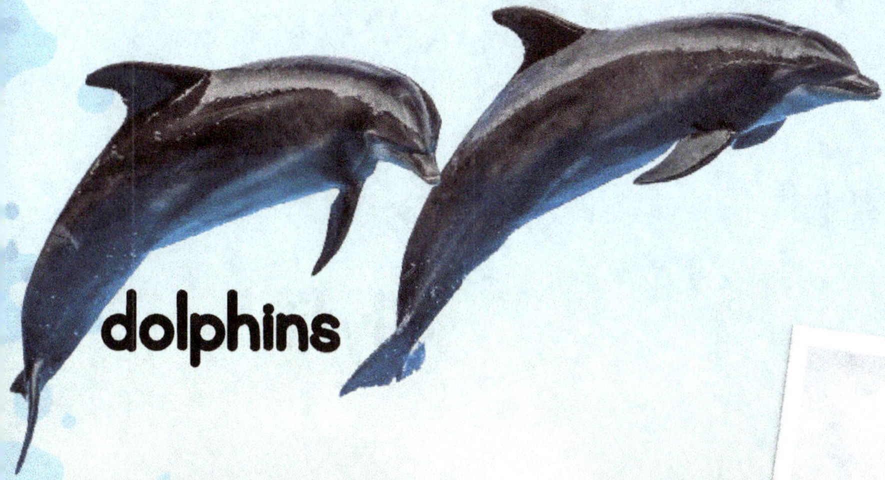

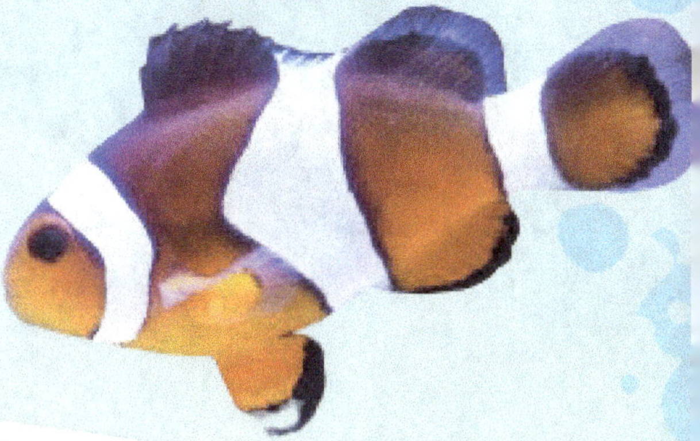

fish

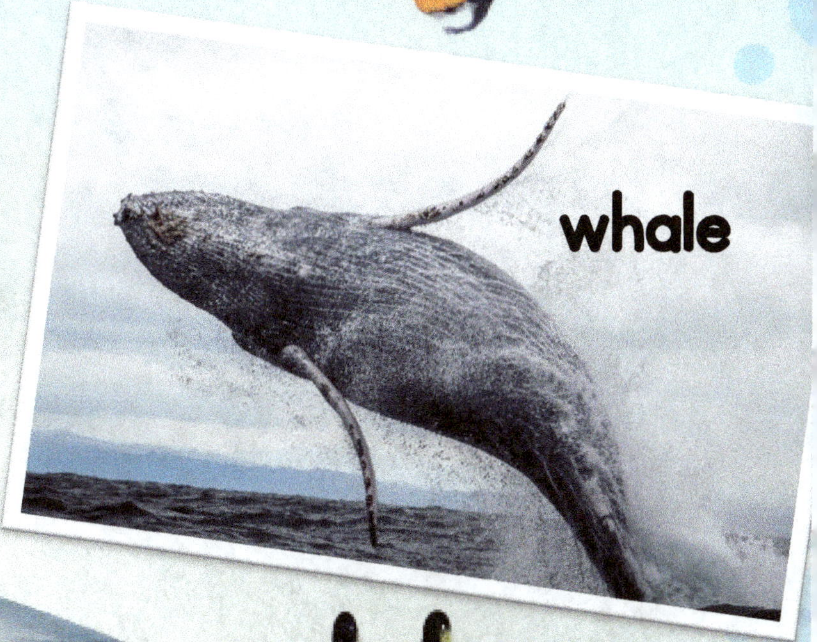

dolphins

Look at all these animals that **live** in **water**!

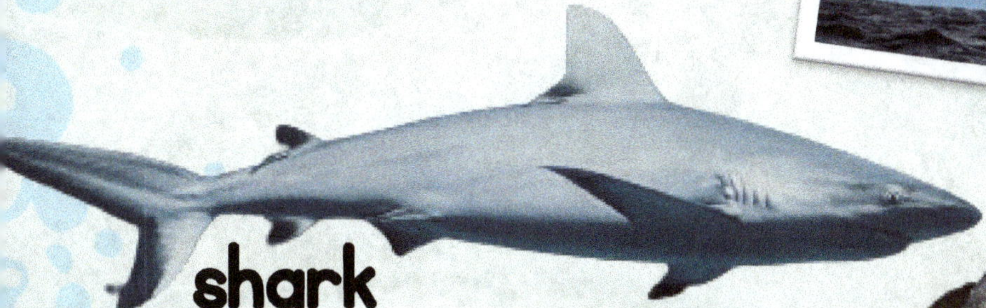

whale

shark

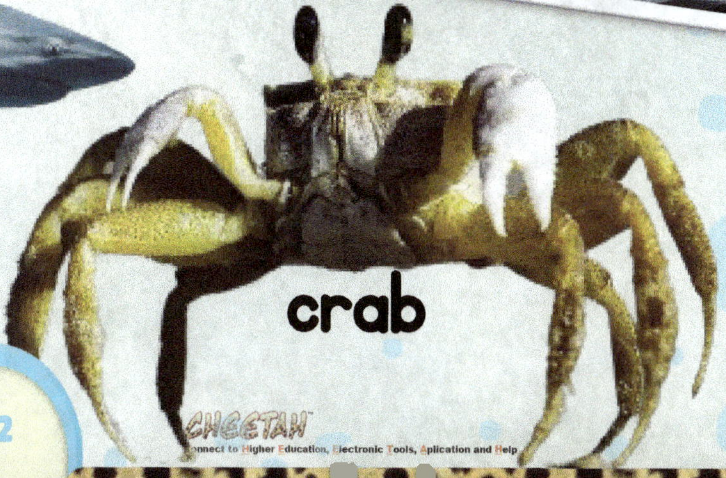

crab

These **fish** are hiding in a plant called coral.

Some plants also **live** in **water**.

Seagrass also grows under **water**.

Water lilies **live** in **water**. Their leaves and flowers **float** on the **top**.

Frogs like to sit on the leaves of water lilies!

So many different plants and animals **live** in **water**!

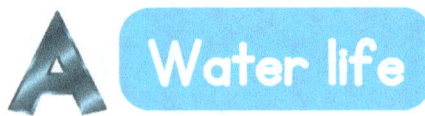

A Water life

Circle all the plants and animals that live in water.

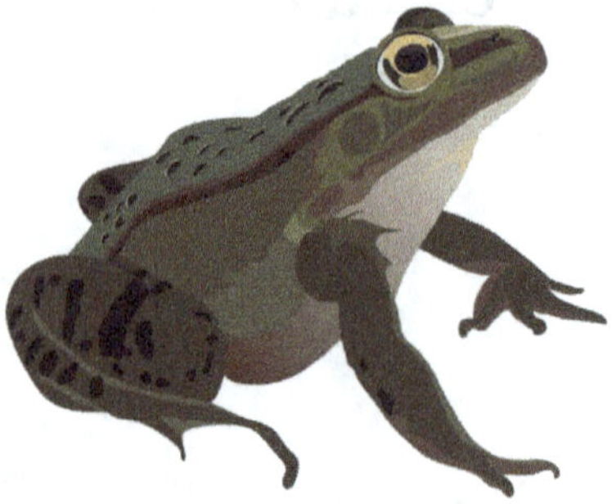

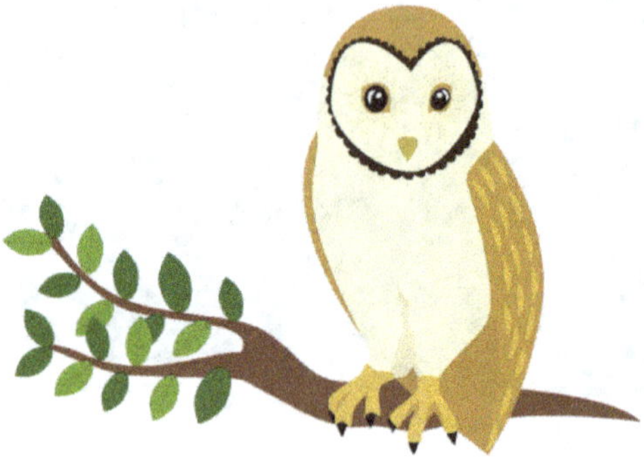

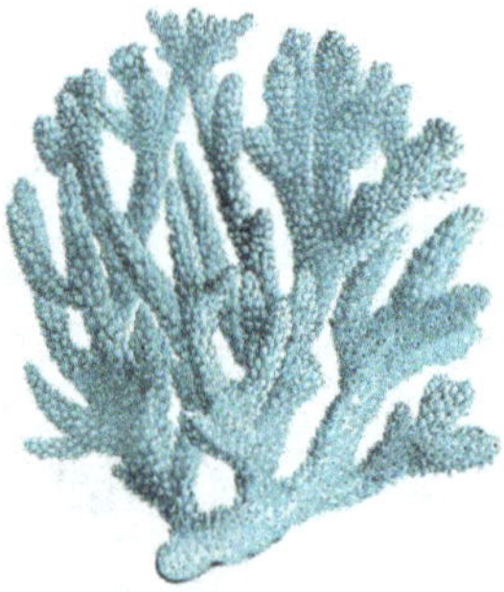

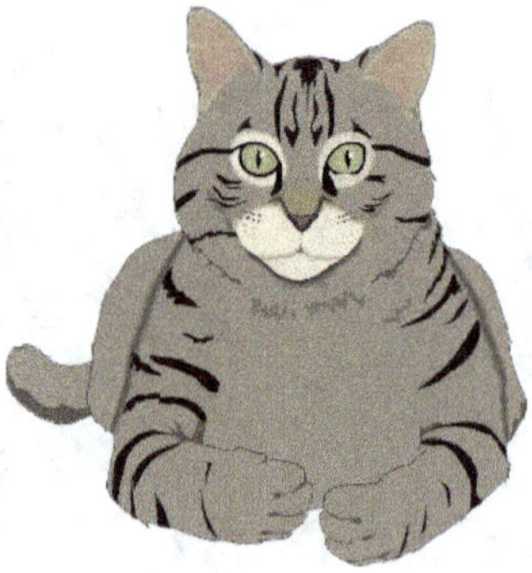

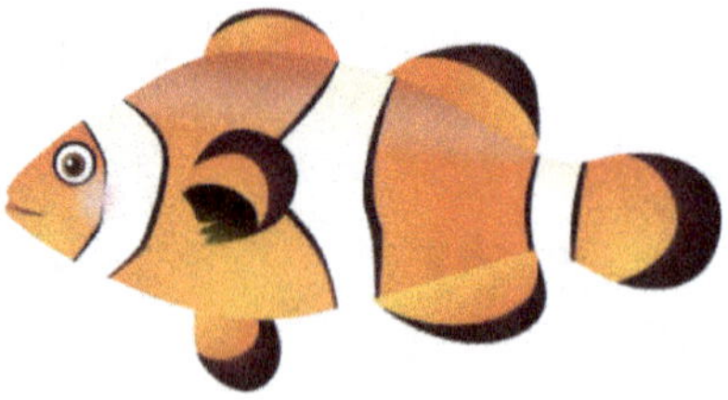

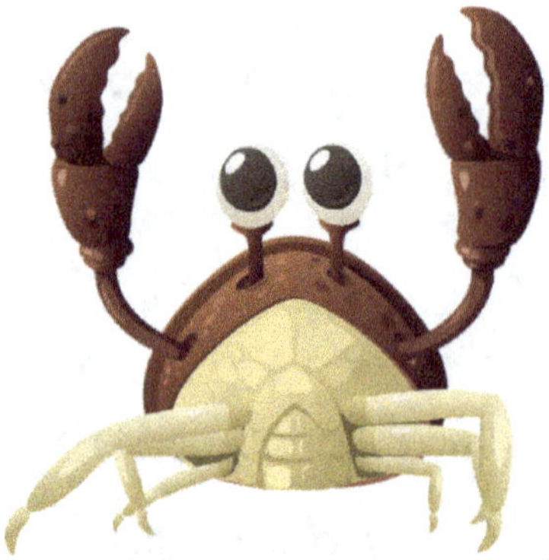

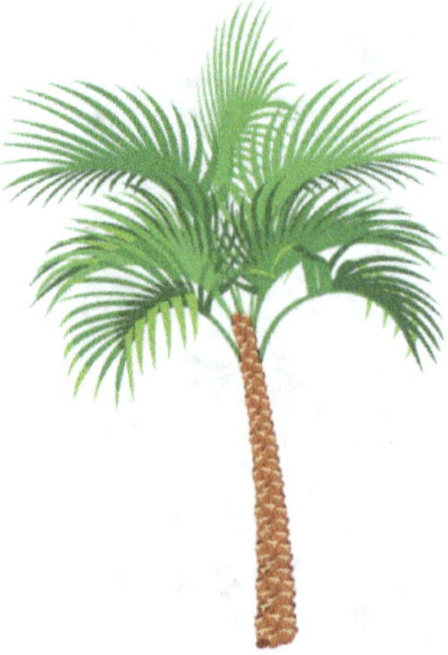

How many animals did you circle? ☐

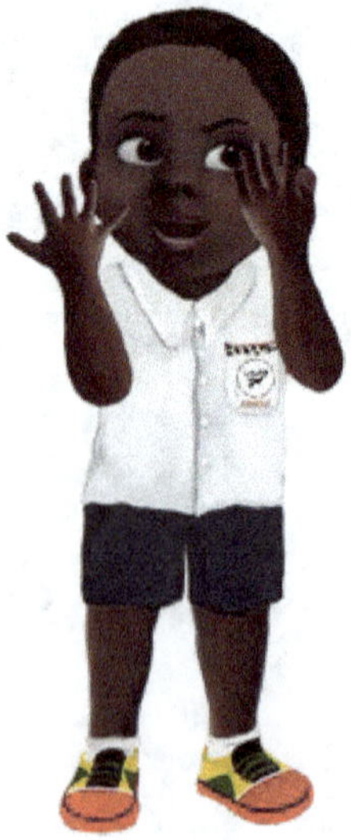

CHEETAH™ Toys & More, LLC Copyright 2022

P Let me do it!
Turtle power!

What you will need:
- child-friendly scissors
- turtle template and paper strips (next pages)
- glue

How to support:
Consider giving pupils the opportunity to practise weaving paper strips with a sheet of old newspaper before beginning the turtle. Always supervise them when cutting and weaving. Note: there are spare paper strips should you need them.

1. Help the pupils to cut out the turtle template.
2. Cut along the dotted lines on the turtle's shell (folding the turtle in half can make this easier).
3. Cut out the lighter green paper strips next.
4. Assist the pupils to weave the paper strips carefully in and out of the slits in the turtle's shell to create a chequerboard pattern.
5. Glue the edges of the paper strips to the edges of the shell, and trim off the excess.
6. Display the pupils' sea turtles.

Learning extension:
Support the pupils in making an underwater background scene of plants that live in water to stick your turtle onto. Can they make other animals that live in water to add to the scene? Take pupils to visit a pond, river or the sea to look for animals that live there e.g. crabs and frogs.

Turtle power turtle template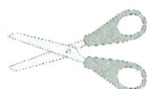

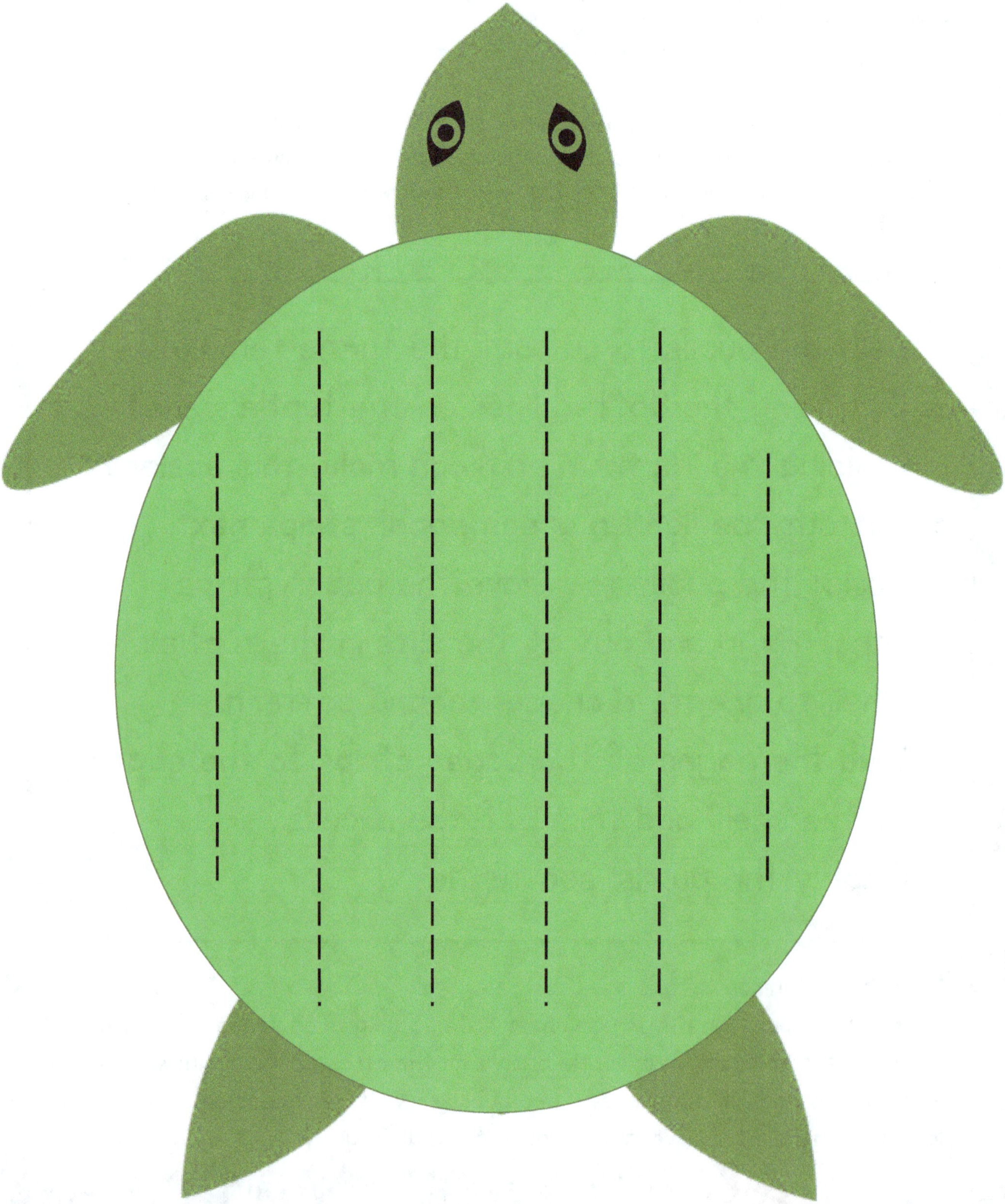

This page has been left blank so you can cut out the turtle template. Remove the page first to make cutting out easier.

Turtle power paper strips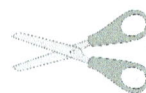

This page has been left blank so you can cut out the paper strips. Remove the page first to make cutting out easier.

Let's rap: Water animals

In water, you will find
creatures and fish of every kind;
You will see little crabs that like to nip,
and frogs that love to jump and skip.

In water, you will find
creatures and fish of every kind;
You will see dolphins, sharks and whales,
And water lilies and shrimps with tails.

In water, you will find
creatures and fish of every kind;
You will see manatees and eels,
a jellyfish and clapping seals.

You will need:
- the *find* and *you* flashcards

How to support:
Show the pupils the *find* flashcard and ask them if they can 'find' and point to some of the animals illustrated on the page. Read the words, directing their attention to the text by having them move their finger along as you read. Read again, this time having the pupils stop on the word *find*. Repeat the 'find game' this time looking for the sight word *you* (as shown on the other flashcard).

Learning extension:
Write out or print the alphabet and ask pupils to locate the letters of the sight word *find*, putting a pebble on each letter. Repeat with the sight word *you*. Cut out the letters that they have found so they can use them to make the two sight words.

 **Water animals: How am I doing?**

Date: _____

Dear Parent:

_____ does/does not fully understand that some animals (e.g. fish, crabs, frogs) and plants live in water. Please review at home. Let us continue to work together.

Signed: _____

Date: _____

Dear Teacher:

Thank you. We have reviewed the concept. My child had a chance to teach me.

Signed: _____

Sticker for mom and/or dad goes here!

Awesome!

_____
(write name here)

understands that some animals (e.g. fish, crabs, frogs) and plants live in water.

Sticker for child goes here!

This page has been left blank so you can cut out the previous page.

 End of chapter: Crack the clues

Together we can!

Work with an adult to complete the crossword.
HINT: The pictures are there to help!

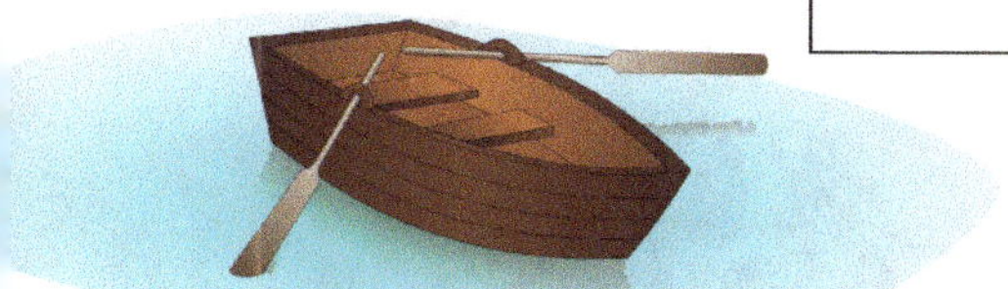

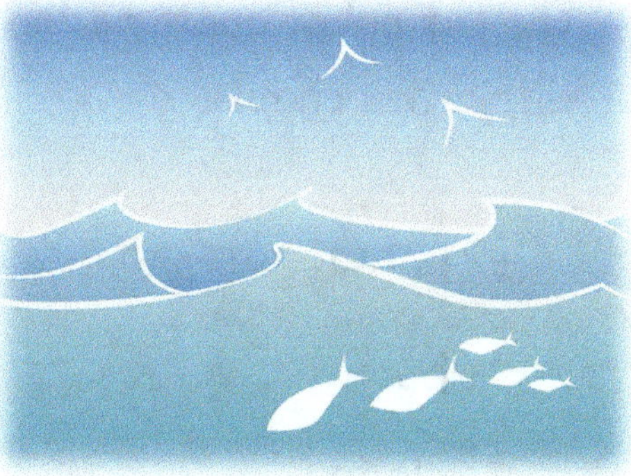

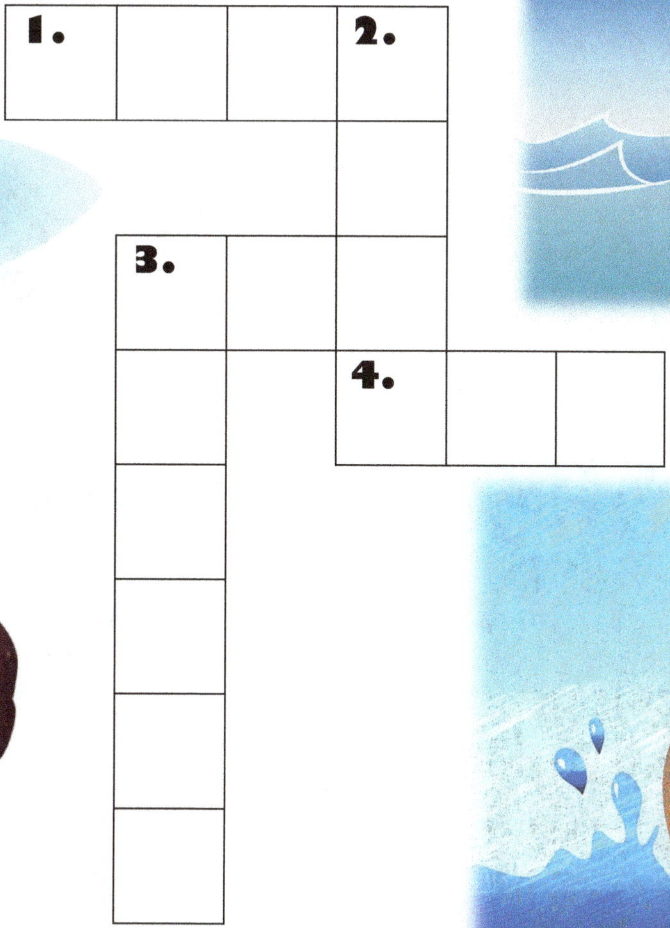

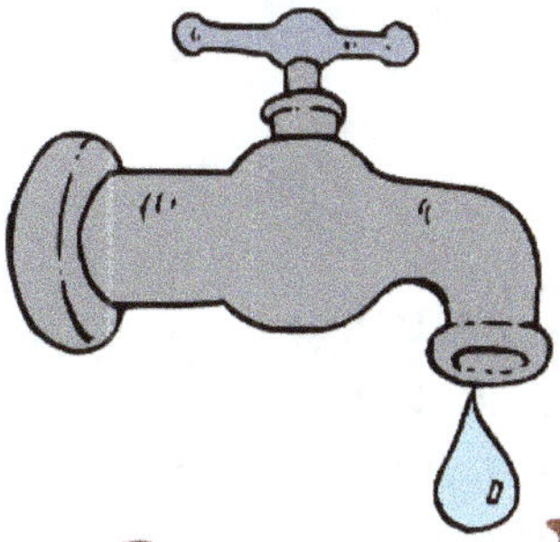

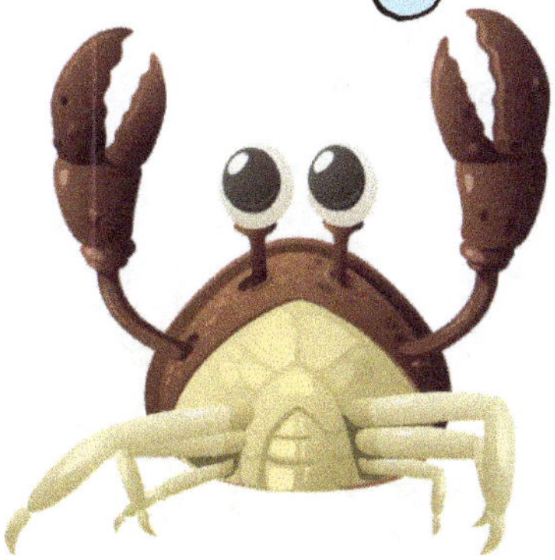

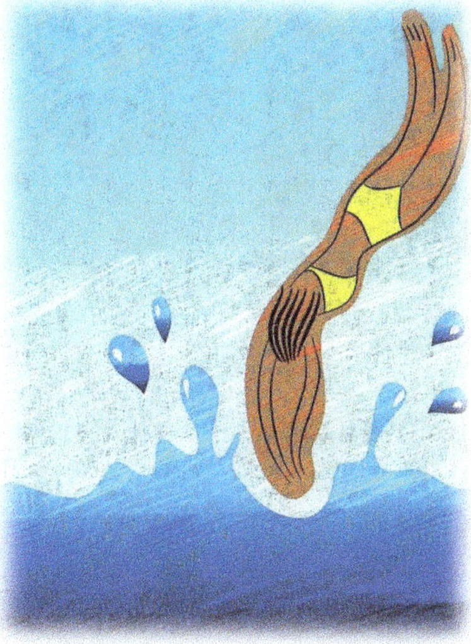

Across
1. This animal with six legs and a hard shell lives in water.
3. This place has lots of water and is found next to sand.
4. You turn this on and water comes out.

Down
2. This floats on top of water and you can sit in it.
3. Water makes this sound when you jump in it.

ANSWERS: **ACROSS:** 1 crab 3 sea 4 tap; **DOWN:** 2 boat 3 splash

Chapter 2: Useful water

Words worth knowing

The list below contains the words from the curriculum that will be discussed within this chapter.

- bubbles
- burn
- clean
- cold
- dirty
- drink
- freeze
- hot
- ice
- lemonade
- melt
- soap
- soapy
- sponge
- warm
- wash
- water

Children will be using these words but should not be expected to spell or memorise them.

Let's talk!
What do you know about how we use water?

How to support:
Look at the picture with the pupils and encourage them to tell you what they see. Ask them to describe what is happening in different areas of the image. Scaffold with prompts such as, '**Can you point to any water? What is the cat/dog/man/boy/girl doing? What are they using water for?**'

Goal:
To have a better understanding of the pupils' existing knowledge about how we use water. Use this knowledge to guide further learning and to complete the first column of the evaluation grid on the next page.

Evaluation grid

This evaluation grid is for teachers and parents. It will help you check the pupil's understanding of the concepts discussed throughout this chapter. Read each statement below and insert a check mark for concepts the pupil has already mastered before the chapter, and then after learning together.

The pupil understands…	Before this chapter	After this chapter
1. people and animals need water to live, and cannot live without water		
2. most animals drink water		
3. water has many uses		
4. water is used for drinking, cooking, cleaning and recreation		
5. we use water to make drinks of different colours and tastes, e.g. lemonade, fruit juices		
6. water can be hot, warm or cold		
7. water put on stove in a pot will get hot		
8. hot water can burn you		
9. water can be frozen to make ice; ice melts to become water		
10. ice feels cold		
11. water keeps us clean		
12. water makes dirty things clean; we use water to bathe ourselves, making us clean		
13. bubbles are made from soap and water		
14. we must not waste water e.g. leave the tap running after use		
15. playing in water is fun; we can have fun with water and in water		
16. some animals love playing in water		
17. water can help us or harm us		

18. we must be careful when playing near water; people can drown in water
19. we must not play in dirty water.

Look out for stars as you learn. These stars will show you which key concept is being taught.

2.1 Life with water

In this section, the pupils will learn that:
- ✓ people and animals need water to live, and cannot live without water
- ✓ most animals drink water
- ✓ water has many uses
- ✓ water is used for drinking, cooking, cleaning and recreation.

C Wonderful water!

Every day we drink water.

Without water, we cannot live.

Most animals drink water too!

People and animals both need water to live.

People use water for lots of other things too.

We use water for cooking food.

We use water for cleaning and washing things.

We even use water for having fun!

A  I need water!

Read the sentence, then tick the picture that goes with it.

I cannot live without water.

☐   ☐   ☐

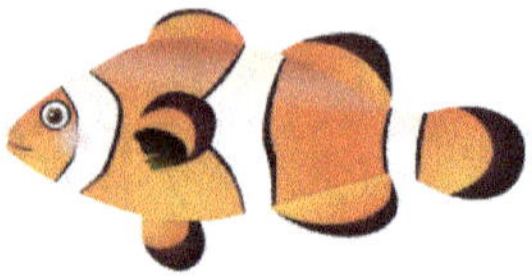

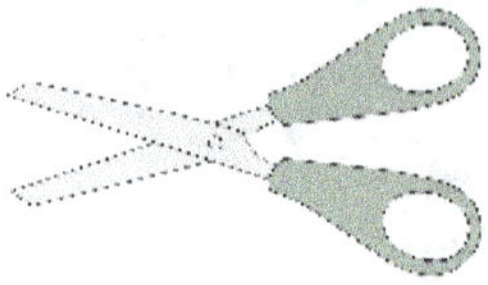

I do not drink water.

☐   ☐   ☐

I do not need water.

☐   ☐   ☐

I drink water.

☐   ☐   ☐

 **What is the use?**

Draw a line to match the picture to the use of water.

   cooking

   washing

   drinking

   swimming

P Let me do it!

Water collage

What you will need:
- a camera OR
- drawing/ colouring supplies and paper
- glue
- child-friendly scissors
- the collage template (over the page)

How to support:
NOTE: If you do not have a camera, the pupils can go to the space where the activity takes place and draw the action instead. Cooking with water is an activity that should be performed by the adult and photographed by pupils. A photograph showing pupils 'having fun' could be taken at a swimming pool, the beach, or in a garden playing with water.

1. Support the pupils in taking a photo of themselves or someone they know using water in as many of these activities as they can:
   - brushing their teeth
   - washing their face
   - drinking
   - washing dishes
   - cooking
   - having fun!
2. Over the page, the pupils should make a collage by gluing the photos around the words to show how they use water in their life.

Learning extension:
Can the pupils think of any more activities that use water? Have them photograph/draw them and add them to their collage. The pupils can also take the camera/drawing supplies on a walk to look for water being used in public places too.

WONDERFUL WATER!

Water collage template

Life with water: How am I doing?

Date: _____

Dear Parent:

_____ does/does not fully understand that people and animals need water to live, and cannot live without water; most animals drink water and water has many uses: drinking, cooking, cleaning and recreation. Please review at home. Let us continue to work together.

Signed: _____

Date: _____

Dear Teacher:

Thank you. We have reviewed the concepts. My child had a chance to teach me.

Signed: _____

Sticker for mom and/or dad goes here!

Wonderful!

_____
(write name here)

understands that people and animals need water to live, and cannot live without water; most animals drink water and water has many uses: drinking, cooking, cleaning and recreation.

Sticker for child goes here!

This page has been left blank so you can cut out the previous page.

2.2 Taste-tastic!

In this section, the pupils will learn that we use water to make drinks of different colours and tastes, e.g. lemonade, fruit juices.

C Delicious drinks

We can use **water** to make yummy **drinks**, of all different colours!

Mixing **water** with sugar and lemons makes **lemonade**.

Fruit juices are made by squeezing juice from fruits and mixing it with **water**.

Orange juice is orange.

Watermelon juice is red.

Water is used to make hot drinks like tea and hot chocolate.

Tea and hot chocolate are brown drinks.

What colour drinks have you tried?

A Thirsty work

Colour the drinks the correct colour.

pineapple juice

tea

watermelon juice

orange juice

Let me do it!

Let's make lemonade

What you will need:
- 1 cup sugar
- glasses
- 1 cup water (for the syrup)
- 6-8 lemons
- a jug
- access to extra water
- a knife
- a saucepan

How to support:
Supervise the pupils at all times during this activity. Allow them to put the sugar and water into the saucepan, then keep them away from the stove while it is heating. Use the words hot, warm, cool and cold to describe the temperature of the different drink elements.

1. Simmer one cup of water and one cup of sugar in a small saucepan.
2. While the mixture is simmering, juice the lemons until you have one cup of juice.
3. When the sugar has completely dissolved to form a syrup, remove the saucepan from the heat.
4. Pour the syrup and lemon juice into a jug and add two to three cups of water.
5. Taste the mixture. Too sweet? Add lemon juice. Too strong? Add water.
6. Place the lemonade in the fridge for around half an hour until cool.
7. Enjoy a glass of lemonade with ice and lemon slices!

Learning extension:
Ask friends and family or look online for other fruit juice recipes. How many different coloured drinks can you make? This is also a sight word opportunity for the *blue*, *red* and *yellow* flashcards.

Drinking water: How am I doing?

Date: _____

Dear Parent:

_____ does/does not fully understand that we use water to make drinks of different colours and tastes, e.g. lemonade, fruit juices. Please review at home. Let us continue to work together.

Signed: _____

Date: _____

Dear Teacher:

Thank you. We have reviewed the concept. My child had a chance to teach me.

Signed: _____

Sticker for mom and/or dad goes here!

Fantastic!

_____
(write name here)

understands that we use water to make drinks of different colours and tastes, e.g. lemonade, fruit juices.

Sticker for child goes here!

This page has been left blank so you can cut out the previous page.

2.3 Feel the heat

In this section, the pupils will learn that:
- ✓ water can be hot, warm or cold
- ✓ water put on stove in a pot will get hot
- ✓ hot water can burn you
- ✓ water can be frozen to make ice; ice melts to become water, ice feels cold.

C Hot and cold

What does water feel like?

Water can be hot, warm or cold.

When we get water from a sink, we can turn on the hot tap or the cold tap.

Water from the hot tap gets warm and then hot. Warm water is great for washing dishes.

Water from the cold tap is perfect for washing your hands.

When someone puts water into a pot and places it on the stove, what happens to the water?

The water in the pot gets very hot!

We use hot water to cook food.

You must never touch hot water!

If you touch hot water, it can burn you.

Holding the pan by the handles stops the hot water from burning our hands.

If water becomes very cold, it freezes.

Frozen water is called ice.

Ice feels cold!

You can put water in the freezer in trays. When it freezes, use the ice to keep your drinks cold.

Frozen water can also make popsicles!

When ice warms up, it melts to become water again.

A  Getting warmer!

Cut out the pictures of water and stick them into the correct column.

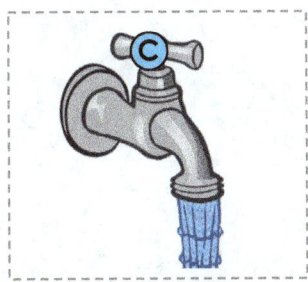  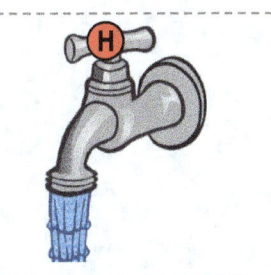

This page has been left blank so you can cut out the picture section. The rest of the page can stay in the book!

 **Let me do it!**

A sweet treat!

What you will need:
- a mango
- a knife and fork
- water
- chocolate or cocoa powder
- empty plastic cups
- ice pop sticks OR plastic spoons
- access to a freezer and stove

How to support:
NOTE: You can substitute the plastic cups for any similar, small plastic container. Supervise the pupils at all times during this activity. Be sure to keep using the words *hot, warm* and *cold* to describe the water. Emphasise that hot water can burn, so you must be very careful making the hot chocolate together.

1. Help the pupils to chop the mango into small pieces. Add a cup of water and mash with a fork.
2. Have the pupils scoop the mixture into the plastic cups and stand an ice pop stick/plastic spoon in the centre of each cup.
3. Together, put the pots into the freezer.
4. Next, heat a saucepan of water and add cocoa powder/hot chocolate powder, according to the manufacturer's instructions.
5. Wait until the hot chocolate has cooled a little, then drink!
6. Check on the ice pops. Once they freeze, you can enjoy those too!

Learning extension:
Wrap a bottle of hot water and a bottle of frozen water in towels, then place each in a box with the lid on. Put a metal spoon in one of the boxes and leave it for a while. Ask pupils what happens to it. Why? Now try the other box. Encourage the pupils to experiment with other items and reinforce the role of the hot/cold water.

Hot and cold: How am I doing?

Date: _____

Dear Parent:

_____ does/does not fully understand that water can be hot, warm or cold; water put on a stove in a pot will get hot; hot water can burn you; water can be frozen to make ice; ice melts to become water and ice feels cold. Please review at home. Let us continue to work together.

Signed: _____

Date: _____

Dear Teacher:

Thank you. We have reviewed the concepts. My child had a chance to teach me.

Signed: _____

Sticker for mom and/or dad goes here!

You're a star!

_____
(write name here)

understands that water can be hot, warm or cold; water put on a stove in a pot will get hot; hot water can burn you; water can be frozen to make ice; ice melts to become water and ice feels cold.

Sticker for child goes here!

This page has been left blank so you can cut out the previous page.

2.4 From dirty to clean

In this section, the pupils will learn that:
- water keeps us clean
- water makes dirty things clean; we use water to bathe ourselves making us clean
- bubbles are made from soap and water
- we must not waste water e.g. leave the tap running after use.

C Scrub-a-dub!

Water is perfect for making dirty things clean.

We use water to wash our dirty dishes.

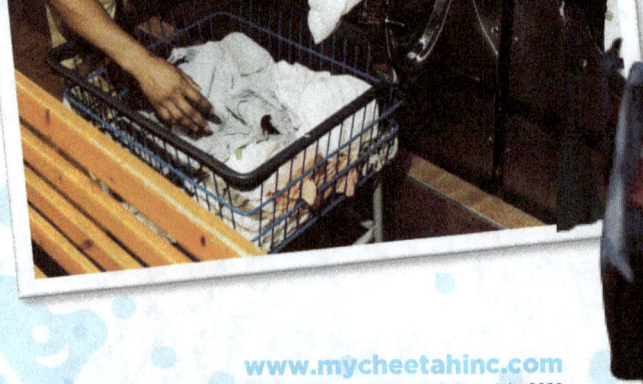

We use water to wash our dirty clothes.

We even use water to wash ourselves!

When we brush our teeth, we use water.

When we are dirty, we use water to bathe or to have a shower.

Water keeps us clean!

If we add soap to water, it makes bubbles!

Soap bubbles help us to make dirty things clean.

We can use a sponge to scrub off dirt.

We must not waste water.

Only use the water you need and remember to turn off the tap!

A  Clean hands

Read the instructions below. Cut out the pictures on the next page and glue them in the correct order.

1.	2.
Wet your hands with water and apply soap.	Rub your hands together in the soap bubbles.

3.	4.
Rinse your hands with water.	Dry your hands.

Clean hands instruction pictures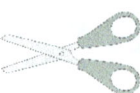

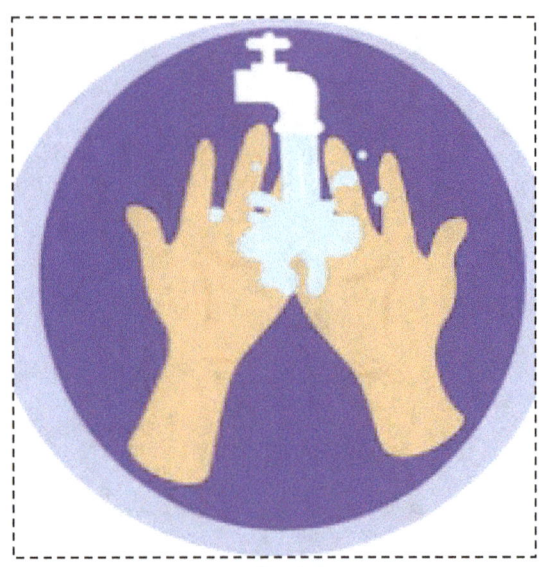

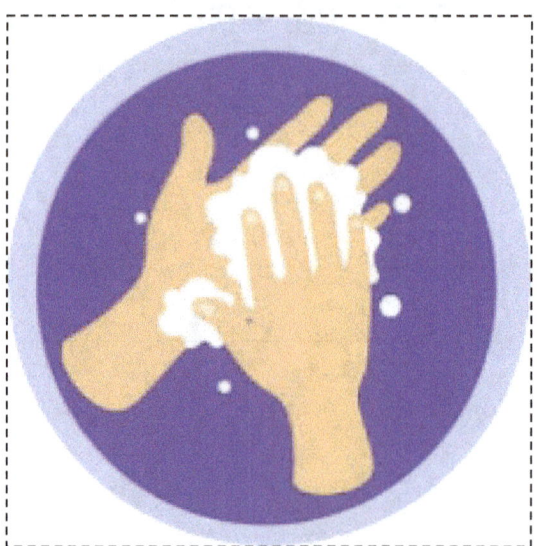

This page has been left blank so you can cut out the instruction pictures. Remove the page first to make cutting out easier.

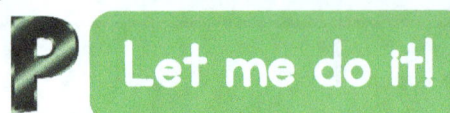

Toy wash

What you will need:
- large tubs
- dishwashing soap
- plastic toys (or other waterproof plastic objects)
- a sponge/scrubbing brush
- warm water
- large towels

How to support:
Before you begin, you may want to put the toys into some wet dirt so they are obviously dirty. An easy alternative to plastic toys is plastic bowls/cups/utensils. As you are filling the tubs, emphasise to the pupils the importance of turning the tap off. Allow them to wash the toys as they wish and play with them in the water if they want to. The pupils may want to physically dry the toys with the towel, and that's fine too!

1. Place pupils in groups. Each group should have two large plastic tubs with warm water.
2. Allow the pupils to help you fill the plastic tubs.
3. Have the pupils lay out a towel beside the tubs.
4. They can then add dishwashing soap to a tub of warm water and swish it around to make bubbles.
5. Ask the pupils to choose dirty toys to wash in the soapy water. They can use a sponge or a scrubbing brush to make the toys clean.
6. The pupils should then rinse the soapy bubbles from the now clean toys in the tubs of water.
7. They can set the toys on the towel to dry.
8. The pupils can continue until all the toys are clean!

Learning extension:
Set up a pretend play 'laundry day', using similar tubs for washing clothes/towels, as well as a washing line and pegs for drying the clean items. With the pupils, make a bubble mixture using 50 ml of dishwashing liquid and 300 ml of water. They can dip a drinking straw into the mixture and blow through it to create bubbles!

 **Let's rap: Water, wash!**

Water, water, wash us please.
Scrub the dirt off muddy knees.
Scrub our skin and clean our feet.
A bubble bath is such a treat!

Soap and bubbles clean with ease,
and clear the plates of rice and peas!
Wash the dishes, every pot and pan.
Leave the kitchen spick and span.

Water, water, wash us please.
Scrub the dirt off muddy knees.
Scrub our skin and clean our feet.
A bubble bath is such a treat!

You will need:
- the *the* sight word flashcard
- a coloured pencil

How to support:
Look at the page together. Read the words, directing the pupils' attention to the text by asking them to guide with their finger as you read. Read again, this time coming up with actions to perform along with the rap (e.g, rubbing knees to show scrubbing the mud off). Look at the *the* flashcard and show the pupils how to form the letters with their finger in the air. Have the pupils find and circle the word *the* in the rap.

Learning extension:
In a shallow tray, mix some dirt and water to make a layer of mud. Show the pupils how to write the sight word *the* in the mud, using their finger. After the pupils erase and practise multiple times, scrub the tray and hands with soap and water, like in the rap!

Water cleans: How am I doing?

Date: _____

Dear Parent:

_____ does/does not fully understand that water keeps us clean and makes dirty things clean; we use water to bathe ourselves, making us clean; bubbles are made from soap and water; we must not waste water e.g. leave the tap running after use. Please review at home. Let us continue to work together.

Signed: _____

Date: _____

Dear Teacher:

Thank you. We have reviewed the concepts. My child had a chance to teach me.

Signed: _____

Sticker for mom and/or dad goes here!

Excellent!

_____
(write name here)

understands that water keeps us clean and makes dirty things clean; we use water to bathe ourselves, making us clean; bubbles are made from soap and water; we must not waste water e.g. leave the tap running after use.

Sticker for child goes here!

2.5 Water fun

In this section, the pupil will learn that:
- ✓ playing in water is fun; we can have fun with water and in water
- ✓ some animals love playing in water
- ✓ water can help us or harm us
- ✓ we must be careful when playing near water; people can drown in water
- ✓ we must not play in dirty water.

C Make a splash!

We can have lots of fun with water!

We can splash and play.

We can even get into the water!

Some animals love playing in water, too!

Do you like to play in water?

We have learned about many ways that water can help us.

But we must remember, water can harm us too.

People can drown in water, so we must be careful when playing near it or in it.

The sea can become rough, or it may be difficult to get out of the pool.

Playing in dirty water can make you ill.

Always play in clean water with an adult close by.

A  Fun in the pool

Colour the picture according to the numbers, then trace the words beneath.

1 = yellow   2 = blue   3 = brown   4 = black

Playing in clean
water is fun!

 **Fun, helpful or harmful?**

Cut out the squares on the next page, then glue them in the correct column.

fun water	helpful water	harmful water

Fun, helpful or harmful cut-outs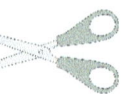

 a dog playing in water	 washing clothes in water	 playing in dirty water
 swimming in water with an adult nearby	 cooking rice in water	 swimming in a storm
 swimming alone	 splashing in clean water	 drinking water

This page has been left blank so you can cut out squares.
Remove the page first to make cutting out easier.

P | Let me do it!

Buckets of fun!

What you will need:
- multiple teams of 4-5 players
- buckets filled with water
- large containers
- large sponges
- some towels

How to support:
Pupils can get very excited playing this game, so set some safety rules before you begin about slippery ground, etc. Feel free to adjust the distance between the buckets and empty containers, and also the size of the empty containers — the larger the container, the longer the pupils will play.

1. Position the two buckets of water to form a start line, with the empty containers set approximately ten metres away.
2. Each team should stand behind a different bucket of water, with one player in each team holding the sponge.
3. On a signal to begin, the sponge holders should soak up water from the bucket, then run to the empty container and squeeze the water into it before running back to the bucket.
4. It is then the next player's turn to do the same.
5. Play continues until one team wins by filling their container with water first.

Learning extension:
Play "Sponge Toss" by setting the buckets of water opposite each other and having a pupil stand at each bucket. The pupils can take turns to soak up some water and throw the wet sponge to – or at – the pupil opposite. Show the pupil the flashcard showing the sight word *play* and have them squeeze water from the sponge to form the letters on the ground.

 **Water fun: How am I doing?**

Date: _____

Dear Parent:

_____ does/does not fully understand that playing in water is fun; we can have fun with water and in water; some animals love playing in water; water can help us or harm us; we must be careful when playing near water; people can drown in water; we must not play in dirty water. Please review at home. Let us continue to work together.

Signed: _____

Date: _____

Dear Teacher:

Thank you. We have reviewed the concepts. My child had a chance to teach me.

Signed: _____

Sticker for mom and/or dad goes here!

Congratulations!

_____

(write name here)

★ understands that playing in water is fun; we can have fun with water and in water; some animals love playing in water; water can help us or harm us; we must be careful when playing near water; people can drown in water; we must not play in dirty water.

Sticker for child goes here!

This page has been left blank so you can cut out the previous page.

Let's rap: Useful Water

Put water in a pot.
For drinking tea, we make it hot.
Splish, splosh, splash!
Cleaning dishes in a flash!

When frozen, water makes ice.
It cools our drinks that taste quite nice.
Splosh, splash and splish!
Water is perfect for steaming fish.

We use water to clean our dirty clothes.
Or wash our windows with a hose.
Splosh, splish, splash!
Water gives our bodies a wash!

You will need:
- the *a* sight word flashcard
- two differently coloured pencils

How to support:
Look at the pictures on the page with the pupils – ask what they have to do with water. Lay the flashcard down on the page, then have the pupils move the card down as you read each line. Look at the word *a* on the flashcard. Explain that it is a letter but also a word. Help pupils find the letter 'a' in the rap and colour it wherever they see it. Read the rap again, and have the pupils use another colour to circle the word *a* wherever it occurs.

Learning extension:
Further explore the *sh* sound in the words 'splish, splash, splosh' by heading to the beach so the pupils can 'splish, spash and splosh' in the water, then collect shells and arrange them to form the letters 'sh' on the sand.

 **End of chapter: Crack the clues**

Together we can!

Work with an adult to complete the crossword.
HINT: The pictures are there to help!

Across
3. Make these by mixing soap and water.
5. This brown drink is made with hot water.

Down
1. This name is given to frozen water.
2. Make this drink by mixing fruit and water.
4. We use this to make bubbles to wash with.

ANSWERS: ACROSS: 3 bubbles 5 tea; DOWN: 1 ice 2 juice 4 soap

RESOURCES

# Sight words activities

Note: Each of the following activities can be carried out with any number of sight words, from 2-20, depending on the pupil's previous learning.

Bang it!
Lay the flashcards out on different kitchen implements that can be banged with a wooden spoon (e.g. a mixing bowl, a saucepan and so on). Call out a word, then the pupil must find it and bang it with the spoon! Can you make a rhythm together?

Post it!
Make a post box by cutting a thin, rectangular opening into a box that closes. Lay the flashcards out. Call out a word, then the pupil must find it and post it in the box!

Swat it!
Lay the flashcards out. Call out a word, then the pupil must find it and swat it with their hand, a rolled-up newspaper, or a fly swatter!

Discover it!
Lay the flashcards out, then cover them with a thin layer of sand. The pupil can gently brush away the sand with a paintbrush to 'discover' each word.

Write it!
Put a small amount of paint into a plastic bag that seals along the top. Lay the bag out flat, with the paint evenly spread, and allow the pupil to practise 'writing' sight words by moving their finger over the paint.

Roll it!
Assign six flashcards with the numbers 1-6. Have the pupil roll a die, then write the word that the number corresponds to.

Type it!
Practise typing the words on a computer keyboard.

Sight words flash cards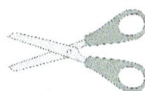

a	and
big	blue
come	find
go	in
is	it

This page has been left blank so you can cut out the flash cards.
Remove the page first to make cutting out easier.

www.ingramcontent.com/pod-product-compliance
Lightning Source LLC
Chambersburg PA
CBHW082209070526
44585CB00020B/2352

Sight words flash cards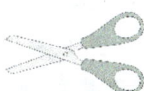

little	look
play	red
see	the
to	we
yellow	you

This page has been left blank so you can cut out the flash cards.
Remove the page first to make cutting out easier.